Ninja Smoothie Revolution: 100 Recipes for Weight Loss and Increased Energy

De Flavor Fusion

Copyright © 2023 De Flavor Fusion
All rights reserved.
:

Contents

INTRODUCTION 7
1. Green Power Ninja Smoothie 9
2. Berry Blast Ninja Smoothie 9
3. Tropical Energy Ninja Smoothie 10
4. Chocolate Peanut Butter Ninja Smoothie 11
5. Mango Ginger Ninja Smoothie 12
6. Blueberry Spinach Ninja Smoothie 13
7. Pineapple Coconut Ninja Smoothie 13
8. Kale and Avocado Ninja Smoothie 14
9. Strawberry Kiwi Ninja Smoothie 15
10. Almond Butter Banana Ninja Smoothie 15
11. Spinach Mango Ninja Smoothie 16
12. Raspberry Chia Ninja Smoothie 17
13. Orange Carrot Ninja Smoothie 17
14. Cucumber Mint Ninja Smoothie 18
15. Peanut Butter Chocolate Banana Ninja Smoothie 19
16. Watermelon Lime Ninja Smoothie 20
17. Mixed Berry Protein Ninja Smoothie 20
18. Pineapple Kale Ninja Smoothie 21
19. Mango Pineapple Ninja Smoothie 22
20. Berry Beet Ninja Smoothie 22
21. Green Apple Spinach Ninja Smoothie 23
22. Papaya Coconut Ninja Smoothie 24
23. Blueberry Almond Ninja Smoothie 25
24. Strawberry Banana Ninja Smoothie 25
25. Kiwi Spinach Ninja Smoothie 26
26. Chocolate Peanut Butter Banana Ninja Smoothie 27
27. Orange Mango Ninja Smoothie 28

28. Cucumber Green Ninja Smoothie 29

29. Pineapple Mango Coconut Ninja Smoothie 29

30. Peach Raspberry Ninja Smoothie 30

31. Almond Joy Ninja Smoothie 31

32. Watermelon Berry Ninja Smoothie 32

33. Spinach Mango Coconut Ninja Smoothie 32

34. Raspberry Coconut Ninja Smoothie 33

35. Carrot Ginger Ninja Smoothie 34

36. Mixed Berry Spinach Ninja Smoothie 35

37. Green Tea Matcha Ninja Smoothie 35

38. Pineapple Orange Ninja Smoothie 36

39. Blueberry Peach Ninja Smoothie 37

40. Kiwi Pineapple Spinach Ninja Smoothie 38

41. Chocolate Cherry Ninja Smoothie 38

42. Mango Banana Coconut Ninja Smoothie 39

43. Strawberry Watermelon Ninja Smoothie 40

44. Cucumber Avocado Ninja Smoothie 41

45. Peanut Butter Banana Protein Ninja Smoothie 41

46. Orange Raspberry Ninja Smoothie 42

47. Spinach Pineapple Ninja Smoothie 43

48. Raspberry Mango Ninja Smoothie 44

49. Carrot Apple Ginger Ninja Smoothie 45

50. Mixed Berry Greek Yogurt Ninja Smoothie 45

51. Green Goddess Ninja Smoothie 46

52. Pineapple Banana Ninja Smoothie 47

53. Blueberry Pomegranate Ninja Smoothie 48

54. Kiwi Berry Ninja Smoothie 48

55. Chocolate Mint Ninja Smoothie 49

56. Watermelon Berry Mint Ninja Smoothie 50

57. Mango Spinach Coconut Ninja Smoothie 51
58. Strawberry Mango Chia Ninja Smoothie 52
59. Cucumber Celery Green Ninja Smoothie 52
60. Peanut Butter Chocolate Protein Ninja Smoothie 53
61. Orange Pineapple Ginger Ninja Smoothie 54
62. Spinach Blueberry Ninja Smoothie 55
63. Raspberry Peach Ninja Smoothie 55
64. Carrot Orange Ninja Smoothie 56
65. Mixed Berry Oatmeal Ninja Smoothie 57
66. Green Avocado Ninja Smoothie 58
67. Pineapple Coconut Lime Ninja Smoothie 58
68. Blueberry Banana Ninja Smoothie 59
69. Kiwi Green Apple Ninja Smoothie 60
70. Chocolate Hazelnut Ninja Smoothie 61
71. Watermelon Mint Lime Ninja Smoothie 61
72. Mango Banana Spinach Ninja Smoothie 62
73. Cherry Almond Ninja Smoothie 63
74. Green Matcha Ninja Smoothie 64
75. Dragon Fruit Berry Ninja Smoothie 64
76. Peach Mango Ginger Ninja Smoothie 65
77. Pineapple Spinach Coconut Ninja Smoothie 66
78. Raspberry Coconut Chia Ninja Smoothie 67
79. Carrot Turmeric Ginger Ninja Smoothie 67
80. Spirulina Blueberry Ninja Smoothie 68
81. Mango Pineapple Ginger Ninja Smoothie 69
82. Banana Oatmeal Ninja Smoothie 70
83. Mixed Berry Kale Ninja Smoothie 70
84. Watermelon Cucumber Mint Ninja Smoothie 71
85. Cherry Vanilla Almond Ninja Smoothie 72

86. Avocado Lime Ninja Smoothie 73
87. Spinach Mango Banana Ninja Smoothie 73
88. Coconut Berry Ninja Smoothie 74
89. Pineapple Orange Ginger Ninja Smoothie 75
90. Green Kiwi Ninja Smoothie 75
91. Chocolate Raspberry Ninja Smoothie 76
92. Strawberry Coconut Ninja Smoothie 77
93. Blueberry Acai Ninja Smoothie 78
94. Green Apple Celery Ninja Smoothie 78
95. Peanut Butter Espresso Ninja Smoothie 79
96. Orange Turmeric Ninja Smoothie 80
97. Papaya Lime Mint Ninja Smoothie 81
98. Mango Pineapple Coconut Water Ninja Smoothie 82
99. Raspberry Lime Basil Ninja Smoothie 82
100. Matcha Banana Ninja Smoothie 83
CONCLUSION 85

INTRODUCTION

Welcome to the Ninja Smoothie Revolution! A revolution that has been created to help you make delicious and nutritious smoothies which can aid in weight loss and increase your energy levels.

This cookbook provides 100 recipes that are designed to be used in smoothies which will not only taste great but will also help you reach your goals. The smoothies featured in this cookbook are chock-full of fruits and vegetables, blended with wholesome ingredients like yogurt and nut butters, and even spices and herbal ingredients that are sure to give you the nutritious kick you need to stay energized and healthy. From classic smoothie recipes to more inventive creations, you'll be sure to find the perfect recipe to fill even the pickiest of eaters.

Smoothies are a great way to get your daily nutrients without having to take a bunch of supplements. The nutrient-rich fruits and vegetables featured in this cookbook provide your body with the vitamins, minerals, and fiber that it needs to stay healthy. And with recipes like those in this cookbook, you can enjoy delicious smoothies that will make it easy for you to get your vitamins and minerals, as well as aid your weight loss goals if you choose to use this cookbook in your weight-loss program.

In addition to the delicious recipes, this cookbook also includes helpful tips and tricks for making the perfect smoothie. We'll cover topics such as what type of blender to use, how to choose the freshest fruits and vegetables, how to properly prepare the ingredients, and even some ideas for creative smoothie creations. With this book, you can easily learn the basics of creating nutritious and delicious smoothies to fit your lifestyle.

So, what are you waiting for? Dive into the Ninja Smoothie Revolution and begin your journey to a healthier, happier, and more energized you! With this cookbook, you'll learn how to make delicious and nutritious smoothies with ease. You'll be creating mouth-watering smoothies in no time! So, let's get blending, and enjoy the Ninja Smoothie Revolution!

1. Green Power Ninja Smoothie

This Green Power Ninja Smoothie is a delicious and nutritious way to fuel your day. Packed with fruits and vegetables, this smoothie will give you all the energy you need to conquer your day like a ninja!
Serving: 1-2
Preparation time: 5 minutes
Ready time: 5 minutes

Ingredients:
- 1 banana
- 2 cups spinach
- 1 cup frozen mixed berries
- ½ cup plain Greek yogurt
- 1 cup almond milk
- 1 teaspoon honey

Instructions:
1. Place all Ingredients in a blender and blend until smooth.
2. Pour the smoothie into a glass.
3. Enjoy your Green Power Ninja Smoothie!

Nutrition information:
Calories: 222 kcal, Carbohydrates: 37.3 g, Protein: 9.7 g, Fat: 6.4 g, Fiber: 5.9 g, Sugar: 21.8 g.

2. Berry Blast Ninja Smoothie

Start your day right with this Berry Blast Ninja Smoothie! Blending fresh fruit, protein, and dairy, this smoothie is a great tasting drink that will keep you going throughout the morning.
Serving: 2
Preparation time: 10 minutes
Ready time: 10 minutes

Ingredients:
- ½ cup fresh or frozen strawberries

- ½ cup fresh or frozen blueberries
- ½ cup fresh or frozen raspberries
- ½ cup 2% plain Greek yogurt
- ¼ cup rolled oats
- ½ cup ice cubes
- 2 tablespoons honey
- ¼ cup almond milk

Instructions:
1. In a blender, combine all Ingredients and blend until smooth.
2. Serve immediately.

Nutrition information: per serving – Calories: 144, Fat: 2.5g, Carbohydrates: 26g, Protein: 5.6g, Sodium: 21mg, Fiber: 5.8g

3. Tropical Energy Ninja Smoothie

Start every morning with this energizing and delicious Tropical Energy Ninja Smoothie. Perfectly balanced, this smoothie will give your body a well-deserved boost of vitamins and minerals to keep you up and running throughout the day.
Serving: 4
Preparation time: 5 minutes
Ready time: 5 minutes

Ingredients:
- 1 banana
- 1 cup frozen mango
- 1/2 cup pineapple
- 1/4 cup spinach leaves
- 1/2 cup coconut water
- 2 tablespoons chia seeds
- 2 tablespoons protein powder

Instructions:
1. Place all Ingredients in a blender and blend on high speed for 1-2 minutes until creamy and smooth.
2. Serve in tall glasses or glasses with a straw and enjoy immediately.

Nutrition information:
- Calories: 180
- Total Fat: 4g
- Saturated Fat: 2g
- Cholesterol: 0mg
- Sodium: 86mg
- Carbohydrates: 29g
- Fiber: 6g
- Sugar: 13g
- Protein: 6g

4. Chocolate Peanut Butter Ninja Smoothie

This Chocolate Peanut Butter Ninja Smoothie is creamy, delicious, and perfect for a quick breakfast, snack or even dessert!
Serving: 2
Preparation time: 5 minutes
Ready time: 5 minutes

Ingredients:
-1 cup of your favorite plant-based milk
-1 banana
-2 tablespoons cocoa powder
-2 tablespoons peanut butter
-1 tablespoon honey
-1/2 teaspoon ground cinnamon
-3 teaspoons chia seeds

Instructions:
1. Place the plant-based milk, banana, cocoa powder, peanut butter, honey, and cinnamon in a blender and blend until smooth.
2. Add in the chia seeds and give it one last blend. If the mixture is too thick, add a bit more plant-based milk to thin it out.
3. Pour into two glasses and enjoy.

Nutrition information: Calories 426, Total Fat 18g, Saturated Fat 4g, Trans Fat 0g, Cholesterol 0mg, Sodium 15mg, Total

Carbohydrate 58g, Dietary Fiber 9g, Total Sugars 34g, Includes 23g Added Sugars, Protein 16g.

5. Mango Ginger Ninja Smoothie

This nutritious and delicious Mango Ginger Ninja Smoothie is a perfect way to kick off the day. Its creamy texture and sweet, spicy flavour is sure to make it a favorite!
Serving: 2
Preparation Time: 10 minutes
Ready Time: 10 minutes

Ingredients:
-1 cup of frozen mango
-1 fresh banana
-1 tablespoon fresh ginger, grated
-1/3 cup of plain yogurt
-1 cup of almond milk
-1 teaspoon of honey

Instructions:
1. In a blender, add the frozen mango, banana, ginger, yogurt, almond milk, and honey.
2. Blend the Ingredients together on a high speed until smooth.
3. Pour the smoothie into two glasses, and enjoy!

Nutrition information:
Calories: 240
Total Fat: 5.5 grams
Saturated Fat: 0.7 grams
Cholesterol: 2.3 milligrams
Sodium: 55.9 milligrams
Carbohydrates: 43.3 grams
Fiber: 3.3 grams
Sugar: 31.2 grams
Protein: 5.2 grams

6. Blueberry Spinach Ninja Smoothie

Enjoy a healthy and delicious smoothie packed full with nutrients from the blueberries and spinach. This blueberry spinach ninja smoothie is a true superpower of a smoothie that will make you ready for anything that comes along your way!
Serving: 2
Preparation time: 5 mins
Ready time: 5 mins

Ingredients:
- ½ cup blueberries
- 1 banana
- 2 cups baby spinach
- 1 tablespoon chia seeds
- ½ cup almond milk
- 1 cup ice

Instructions:
1. Add all the Ingredients to your blender.
2. Blend until you reach a smooth and creamy consistency.
3. Pour into two glasses and serve with a chilled straw.

Nutrition information:
Calories: 180 kcal; Fat: 4 g; Carbohydrates: 37 g; Protein: 5 g; Fiber: 8 g.

7. Pineapple Coconut Ninja Smoothie

Enjoy a vacation-inspired Pineapple Coconut Ninja Smoothie that is filled with flavor, nutrition, and healthy fats. This delicious smoothie is a great way to start your day or to refuel after a workout.
Serving: 4
Preparation Time: 5 minutes
Ready Time: 5 minutes

Ingredients:
- 2 cups frozen pineapple
- 2 frozen bananas

- 1/2 cup coconut milk
- 1/4 cup full-fat Greek yogurt
- 2 teaspoons honey
- 2 tablespoons unsweetened shredded coconut
- 1 teaspoon coconut extract

Instructions:
1. Add all Ingredients to a blender and blend until smooth.
2. Divide into 4 glasses and enjoy.

Nutrition information:
Calories - 172
Fat - 6 g
Carbohydrates - 28 g
Protein - 4 g
Fiber - 3 g

8. Kale and Avocado Ninja Smoothie

Kale and Avocado Ninja Smoothie is a delicious and nutritious drink that can help you stay full and energized throughout the day. It is easy to make and only takes minutes to put together.
Serving: 2
Preparation Time: 5 minutes
Ready Time: 5 minutes

Ingredients:
- 2 cups of kale
- ½ avocado
- 1 tablespoon of flaxseed
- ½ teaspoon of ginger powder
- 2 cups of pineapple juice

Instructions:
1. In a blender, combine the kale, avocado, flaxseed, and ginger powder. Blend until smooth.
2. Add the pineapple juice and blend until well-combined.
3. Serve immediately or store in the refrigerator for future use.

Nutrition information: Each serving of Kale and Avocado Ninja Smoothie offers approximately 220 calories, 8g of protein, 13g of fiber, 7g of fat, 39g of carbohydrates, and 5g of sugar.

9. Strawberry Kiwi Ninja Smoothie

Enjoy the refreshing taste of summer with this Strawberry Kiwi Ninja Smoothie. Packed full of vitamins and nutrients, this smoothie is sure to keep your energy high throughout the day.
Serving: 1
Preparation time: 5 minutes
Ready time: 5 minutes

Ingredients:
2 cups frozen strawberries, 2 kiwis, 1/2 cup almond milk, 1 banana, 2 tablespoons honey

Instructions:
1. Peel and cut the kiwis into halves and set aside.
2. Peel the banana and mash it in a small bowl with a fork.
3. Add the frozen strawberries, mashed banana, almond milk and honey to the blender.
4. Blend the Ingredients until a thick and creamy consistency is reached.
5. Add the kiwi pieces to the blender and blend for another few seconds to incorporate.
6. Pour the smoothie into a glass and enjoy!

Nutrition information:
Calories: 284, Total Fat: 2g, Saturated Fat: 0g, Cholesterol: 0mg, Sodium: 28mg, Carbohydrates: 66g, Fiber: 11g, Sugar: 43g, Protein: 4g

10. Almond Butter Banana Ninja Smoothie

Enjoy a delicious and creamy smoothie that is loaded with protein and full of flavor with this almond butter banana ninja smoothie recipe!
Serving: 2 smoothies

Preparation time: 5 minutes
Ready time: 5 minutes

Ingredients:
1 banana
2 tablespoons of almond butter
1 cup of almond milk
1/2 teaspoon of ground cinnamon
1 tablespoon of honey

Instructions:
1. Put the banana, almond butter, almond milk, cinnamon, and honey in a blender and blend on high speed until smooth.
2. Pour into glasses and serve. Enjoy!

Nutrition information:
Each serving of the Almond Butter Banana Ninja Smoothie contains 238 calories, 10.3g fat, 27.7g carbohydrates, 4.1g protein, and 5.1g fiber.

11. Spinach Mango Ninja Smoothie

This Spinach Mango Ninja Smoothie is an easy-to-make and refreshing drink! It's a great way to get your daily boost of vitamins and minerals.
Serving: 2
Preparation Time: 5 minutes
Ready Time: 5 minutes

Ingredients:
- 1 cup spinach
- 1 mango, peeled and sliced
- ½ cup pineapple juice
- ½ cup coconut water
- Ice cubes

Instructions:
1. Place spinach, mango, pineapple juice, and coconut water into a blender.
2. Puree until smooth.

3. Add ice cubes and blend until they are crushed.
4. Serve and enjoy!

Nutrition information:
Calories: 128, Total Fat: 1g, Saturated Fat: 0g, Cholesterol: 0mg, Sodium: 28mg, Carbohydrates: 28g, Dietary Fiber: 4g, Sugar: 20g, Protein: 2.2g.

12. Raspberry Chia Ninja Smoothie

Enjoy a nutritious raspberry chia smoothie any time of day! This smoothie is loaded with fresh and frozen fruit, chia seeds, and almond milk for a filling and delicious treat.
Serving: Makes about two 8-ounce servings
Preparation Time: 5 minutes
Ready Time: 5 minutes

Ingredients:
- ½ cup frozen raspberries
- ½ cup frozen mango
- ½ frozen banana
- 1 cup almond milk (or other milk of your choice)
- 1 tablespoon chia seeds
- 2 tablespoons honey
- ½ teaspoon vanilla extract

Instructions:
1. Combine all the Ingredients in a blender.
2. Blend the Ingredients until smooth.
3. Enjoy right away or store in the refrigerator for later.

Nutrition information:
One 8-ounce serving contains approximately 126 calories, 2 grams of fat, 24 grams of carbohydrate, 4 grams of protein, and 4 grams of fiber.

13. Orange Carrot Ninja Smoothie

Take the flavors of orange and carrots and combine them in this refreshing smoothie! This Orange Carrot Ninja Smoothie is the perfect way to love your greens.
Serving: Makes 2 smoothies
Preparation Time: 10 minutes
Ready Time: 10 minutes

Ingredients:
1 cup orange juice
1 cup fresh or frozen carrots
1 frozen banana
1/2 teaspoon ground ginger
1 teaspoon honey or maple syrup

Instructions:
1. Place orange juice, carrots, banana, ginger and honey in a blender.
2. Blend the Ingredients on medium-high speed until they are smooth and creamy.

Nutrition information:
Calories: 176, Total Fat: 0.8g, Saturated Fat: 0.1g, Cholesterol: 0mg, Sodium: 29.3mg, Total Carbohydrate: 40.3g, Dietary Fiber: 5.6g, Total Sugars: 23.5g, Proteins: 2.5g.

14. Cucumber Mint Ninja Smoothie

Refresh your day with a cooling and invigorating Cucumber Mint Ninja Smoothie. This combination of cool cucumbers, fresh mint leaves, tart lime, creamy coconut, and cooling spinach will be sure to give you the boost of energy you're looking for!
Serving: 1
Preparation Time: 10 minutes
Ready Time: 10 minutes

Ingredients:
- 1 cucumber, chopped
- 1 cup of fresh spinach
- 1/4 cup fresh mint leaves

- Juice from half of a lime
- 1/2 cup coconut milk
- 1 cup ice cubes

Instructions:
1. In a high-speed blender, add the cucumber, spinach, mint leaves, lime juice, and coconut milk and blend until smooth.
2. Add the ice cubes and blend again until combined.
3. Serve immediately.

Nutrition information: Calories – 132, Fat – 7.6g, Sodium – 17mg, Carbohydrates – 15.6g, Fiber – 5.3g, Sugars – 7.6g, Protein – 2.6g.

15. Peanut Butter Chocolate Banana Ninja Smoothie

Nourishing and delicious, this Peanut Butter Chocolate Banana Ninja Smoothie is the perfect way to start off the day. With a mix of protein, carbohydrates, and healthy fats, everyone can enjoy this delicious smoothie.
Serving: 1
Preparation Time: 5 minutes
Ready Time: 5 minutes

Ingredients:
- ½ frozen banana
- 1 tablespoon of peanut butter
- ¼ cup of yogurt
- 1 tablespoon of cocoa powder
- ½ cup of milk
- 1 teaspoon of honey (optional)

Instructions:
1. Add the frozen banana, peanut butter, yogurt, cocoa powder, and milk to a Ninja blender.
2. Blend until everything is smooth and creamy.
3. Taste and add extra honey if necessary.
4. Pour into a glass and serve immediately.

Nutrition information (per serving): Calories: 227; Total fat: 9.6g; Protein: 8.4g; Carbohydrates: 27.6g; Sodium: 121mg; Cholesterol: 9.2mg; Dietary fiber: 3.4g.

16. Watermelon Lime Ninja Smoothie

This Watermelon Lime Ninja Smoothie is an incredibly refreshing, thirst-quenching smoothie recipe. Its simple flavors and cool texture make for the perfect summertime treat.
Serving: One generous glass
Preparation time: 5 minutes
Ready Time: 5 minutes

Ingredients:
- 2 cups of diced watermelon
- 2 tablespoons fresh lime juice
- 2 tablespoons honey
- 1 cup of crushed ice

Instructions:
- In a blender, blend together diced watermelon until smooth.
- Add the lime juice, honey, and crushed ice.
- Blend until smooth.
- Pour into a glass and serve.

Nutrition information
Calories: 155 kcal, Carbohydrates: 40 g, Protein: 1 g, Fat: 0 g, Sodium: 8 mg, Potassium: 248 mg, Fiber: 1 g, Sugar: 33 g, Vitamin A: 596 IU, Vitamin C: 30 mg, Calcium: 12 mg, Iron: 0.4 mg.

17. Mixed Berry Protein Ninja Smoothie

This Mixed Berry Protein Ninja Smoothie is a delicious and healthy smoothie combo, packed with nutrients and lots of fresh fruits! It's perfect for a nutritious breakfast, snack or post-workout meal.
Serving: 2
Preparation time: 10 minutes

Ready time: 10 minutes

Ingredients:
- ½ cup frozen mixed berries
- ½ frozen banana
- 1 scoop of protein powder
- 1 teaspoon chia seeds
- 1 teaspoon coconut flakes
- Pinch of cinnamon
- ½ cup almond milk

Instructions:
1. Place all the Ingredients into a blender and blitz until smooth.
2. Pour the smoothie into two glasses, and enjoy!

Nutrition information:
Calories: 230 | Protein: 10g | Carbs: 33g | Fat: 6g | Fibre: 9g

18. Pineapple Kale Ninja Smoothie

This Pineapple Kale Ninja Smoothie is a nutritious, easy-to-make smoothie that's sure to kickstart your day right!
Serving: 1
Preparation Time: 5 minutes
Ready Time: 5 minutes

Ingredients:
- ½ cup of freshly chopped kale
- ½ cup diced pineapple
- ½ cup orange juice
- ½ frozen banana
- 1 scoop of whey protein or vegan protein

Instructions:
1. Place the kale, pineapple, orange juice, and banana in a blender.
2. Blend for 30-45 seconds, or until the mixture is smooth.
3. Add the scoop of protein to the smoothie and blend for an additional 10-15 seconds.

4. Pour the smoothie in a glass and enjoy!

Nutrition information: Roughly 200 calories, 30g of carbohydrates, 10g of fat, and 19g of protein.

19. Mango Pineapple Ninja Smoothie

This delicious Mango Pineapple Ninja Smoothie is a perfect choice for breakfast, full of nutrition and flavor.
Serving: 1
Preparation Time: 5 minutes
Ready Time: 5 minutes

Ingredients:
- 1 cup fresh mango
- 1/2 cup pineapple
- 1/4 cup Greek-style yogurt
- 1/2 cup coconut milk
- 2 tablespoons honey
- 1 tablespoon chia seeds

Instructions:
1. In a blender, combine all of the Ingredients and blend until smooth.
2. Pour the smoothie into a glass and enjoy.

Nutrition information (per serving):
Calories: 198, Protein: 5g, Carbs: 36.6g, Total Fat: 5.2g, Fiber: 5.2g, Sugar: 27.5g

20. Berry Beet Ninja Smoothie

Start your day off right with this Berry Beet Ninja Smoothie, featuring a creamy blend of beets, raspberries, bananas, and almond milk. The flavors shine through without being too overpowering, and the texture is extremely smooth and refreshing.
Serving: Makes 2 servings
Preparation time: 10 minutes

Ready time: 10 minutes

Ingredients:
- 2 Medium Beets, peeled and roughly chopped
- 1 1/2 Cups Frozen Raspberries
- 1 Frozen Banana
- 1 Cup Unsweetened Almond Milk
- 2 Tablespoons Honey

Instructions:
1. Add all of the Ingredients to a blender and blend until smooth.
2. Pour the smoothie into glasses.
3. Serve immediately.

Nutrition information:
Per Serving:
- Calories: 188
- Fat: 2g
- Carbohydrates: 38g
- Protein: 4g
- Fiber: 9g

21. Green Apple Spinach Ninja Smoothie

Start your day with a super nutritious green smoothie loaded with the goodness of apples and spinach! This Green Apple Spinach Ninja Smoothie is healthy, delicious and packed with health-giving nutrients.
Serving: 1-2
Preparation Time: 5 minutes
Ready Time: 5 minutes

Ingredients:
- 1 cup spinach
- 1 green apple, cored and chopped
- ½ cup plain Greek yogurt
- ¼ cup almond milk
- ½ teaspoon honey
- 2-3 ice cubes

Instructions:
1. Place all the Ingredients in a blender.
2. Blend until everything is smooth.
3. Pour the smoothie into glasses.
4. Serve and enjoy!

Nutrition information:
- Calories: 150
- Fat: 2g
- Protein: 6g
- Carbs: 24g
- Fiber: 4g

22. Papaya Coconut Ninja Smoothie

Enjoy the tropical flavors of papaya and coconut in this delicious papaya coconut ninja smoothie. Rich in antioxidants, this smoothie is the perfect way to start your day or have as an afternoon pick-me-up.
Serving: 1
Preparation Time: 5 minutes
Ready Time: 5 minutes

Ingredients:
- 1 papaya, diced
- 1 cup coconut milk
- 1 cup ice cubes
- 2 teaspoons honey
- A pinch of ground cinnamon

Instructions:
1. Place the diced papaya, coconut milk, ice cubes, honey and a pinch of ground cinnamon into a blender.
2. Blend until smooth.
3. Pour into a glass and enjoy!

Nutrition information:

Calories: 242, Total Fat: 15 g, Saturated Fat: 12 g, Sodium: 93 mg, Carbohydrates: 26 g, Vitamin A: 572 IU, Vitamin C: 60 mg, Calcium: 45 mg, Iron: 2 mg.

23. Blueberry Almond Ninja Smoothie

This tasty and nutritious Blueberry Almond Ninja Smoothie packs a healthy punch for breakfast or a snack. It takes just minutes to make and full of protein, fibre, vitamins and minerals.
Serving: 1
Preparation time: 5 minutes
Ready time: 5 minutes

Ingredients:
- ½ cup almond milk
- ¼ cup almond butter
- 1 scoop vanilla protein powder
- 2 tablespoons flaxseeds
- 1 banana
- ½ cup blueberries
- ½ teaspoon ground cinnamon

Instructions:
1. Place almond milk, almond butter, protein powder, flaxseeds, banana, blueberries and cinnamon in a blender and puree until smooth.
2. Place in a tall glass and enjoy!

Nutrition information: Per serving: 311 calories, 12g protein, 22g fat, 22g carbohydrates, 8g fibre.

24. Strawberry Banana Ninja Smoothie

This delicious and refreshing Strawberry Banana Ninja Smoothie is a perfect addition to any breakfast! It's easy to make and sure to be loved by all, with its creamy texture and hint of sweetness.
Serving: Makes 2-3 servings
Preparation Time:

Ingredients:
- 1 cup diced frozen strawberries
- 1 large banana, diced
- 1/2 cup almond milk
- 1 tablespoon of honey

Instructions:
1. Combine the diced strawberries and banana in a blender.
2. Add the almond milk and honey and blend until all Ingredients are completely combined.
3. Divide the smoothie among two or three glasses, and enjoy!

Nutrition information:
Calories: 131, Fat: 2g, Sodium: 27mg, Carbohydrates: 28g, Fiber: 3g, Protein: 2g.

25. Kiwi Spinach Ninja Smoothie

Kiwi Spinach Ninja Smoothie is a creative and fun way to start your day with an energizing and nutritious drink.
Serving: 2-3
Preparation Time: 10 minutes
Ready Time: 10 minutes

Ingredients:
- 2 peeled and frozen kiwi fruits
- 1 banana
- 2 cups of baby spinach
- 2 tablespoons of almond butter
- 2 tablespoons of honey
- 1 teaspoon of almond extract
- 1 ½ cups of ice
- ½ cup of nut milk

Instructions:
1. In a blender, add the kiwi fruits, banana, spinach, almond butter, honey, almond extract and ice.
2. Blend all of the Ingredients until smooth.
3. Slowly add the nut milk and continue to blend until the smoothie reaches the desired consistency.
4. Pour the finished smoothie into glasses and let it cool for a few minutes before serving.

Nutrition information:
- Calories: 267
- Total Fat: 7g
- Saturated Fat: 1g
- Sodium: 28mg
- Total Carbohydrate: 47g
- Dietary Fibre: 6g
- Sugar: 33g
- Protein: 6g

26. Chocolate Peanut Butter Banana Ninja Smoothie

This Chocolate Peanut Butter Banana Ninja Smoothie is a quick, easy and healthy treat. It combines creamy peanut butter, banana, cocoa and almond milk in a delicious smoothie that's sure to leave you energized and refreshed. Perfect for breakfast, a snack or a treat on a hot summer day!

Serving: 1
Preparation time: 5 minutes
Ready time: 5 minutes

Ingredients:
-1 large banana
-1/4 cup smooth peanut butter
-2 tablespoons cocoa powder
-1 cup unsweetened almond milk
-1 teaspoon honey (optional)

Instructions:

1. Place banana, peanut butter, cocoa powder, almond milk and honey (if using) into a blender.
2. Blend on high speed for 30-40 seconds until everything is completely smooth.
3. Pour into a glass and enjoy.

Nutrition information:
Calories: 454, Total fat: 24 g, Sodium: 270 mg, Carbohydrates: 46 g, Dietary fiber: 8 g, Sugars: 28 g, Protein: 16 g

27. Orange Mango Ninja Smoothie

Get an instant energy boost with this tangy and refreshing Orange Mango Ninja Smoothie. This smoothie is made with a blend of frozen mangoes, freshly squeezed orange juice, plain yogurt, agave syrup, and orange zest. Enjoy your vitamin-packed smoothie any time of the day!
Serving: Makes 4 servings
Preparation Time: 10 minutes
Ready Time: 10 minutes

Ingredients:
- 2 cups of frozen mangoes
- 1/2 cup freshly squeezed orange juice
- 1/2 cup plain yogurt
- 2 tablespoons agave syrup
- 1/4 teaspoon orange zest

Instructions:
1. In a high-speed blender, combine the frozen mangoes, orange juice, plain yogurt, agave syrup, and orange zest.
2. Blend until everything is combined and the texture is creamy and smooth.
3. Serve the smoothie in 4 glasses and enjoy.

Nutrition information:
- Calories:62
- Carbohydrates: 15 g
- Protein: 2 g

- Fat: 0 g
- Sodium: 11 mg
- Sugar: 11 g

28. Cucumber Green Ninja Smoothie

This delicious Cucumber Green Ninja Smoothie is perfect for those days when you need a light and refreshing beverage. It contains plenty of healthy Ingredients and is a great way to get your daily greens.
Serving: 6
Preparation Time: 10 minutes
Ready Time: 10 minutes

Ingredients:
-2 cups cucumber, peeled and chopped
-1 ripe banana, chopped
-1 cup baby spinach
-1 cup coconut water
-1 cup ice
-1/2 teaspoon ground ginger
-Optional: 1/2 teaspoon honey for sweetness

Instructions:
1. Place the cucumber, banana, spinach, coconut water, ice, and ginger into a blender and blend until smooth.
2. Taste and if desired, add honey for sweetness.
3. Serve immediately in 6 glasses.

Nutrition information: Per serving, this smoothie offers 200 calories, 11.3 g fat, 22.5 g carbohydrates, 4.2 g protein, and 2.3 g dietary fiber.

29. Pineapple Mango Coconut Ninja Smoothie

Start your day off with a tropical twist by trying this delicious Pineapple Mango Coconut Ninja Smoothie. Sweet, tangy and refreshing, this

smoothie is the perfect way to energize and satisfy your morning cravings.
Serving: 2
Preparation time: 5 minutes
Ready time: 5 minutes

Ingredients:
- 1/2 cup ripe pineapple
- 1/2 cup ripe mango
- 1/4 cup coconut milk
- 1/4 cup yogurt
- 1/4 cup ice cubes

Instructions:
1. Place the pineapple, mango, coconut milk, yogurt and ice cubes in a blender, and blend until all of the Ingredients are blended together and the mixture is smooth.
2. Divide the pineapple mango coconut smoothie between two glasses and serve immediately.

Nutrition information
- Calories: 123
- Total fat: 4g
- Cholesterol: 12mg
- Sodium: 28mg
- Potassium: 317mg
- Total carbohydrates: 21g
- Protein: 2g

30. Peach Raspberry Ninja Smoothie

This delicious Peach Raspberry Ninja Smoothie is a sweet and fruity, healthy and refreshing treat.
Serving: Serves 1
Preparation time: 5 minutes
Ready time: 5 minutes

Ingredients:

- 1/2 cup frozen, unsweetened raspberries
- 1 cup almond milk
- 1 cup frozen, diced peaches
- 1 frozen banana
- 1/2 teaspoon ground cinnamon
- 2 tablespoons plain fat free Greek yogurt
- 1/2 teaspoon honey (optional)

Instructions:
1. Place all Ingredients in a blender or food processor.
2. Blend Ingredients until desired consistency is achieved.
3. Pour into a glass and enjoy!

Nutrition information
Calories: 247, Total Fat: 2.7g, Sodium: 134mg, Carbohydrates: 48.3g, Fiber: 7g, Sugars: 31g, Protein: 8.4g.

31. Almond Joy Ninja Smoothie

Sweet and creamy almond joy ninja smoothie is a perfect and refreshing guilt-free treat that can be enjoyed anytime of the day.
Serving: 2
Preparation Time: 5 minutes
Ready Time: 10 minutes

Ingredients:
- 1 ½ cups almond milk
- 1 banana, frozen
- 2 Medjool dates, pitted
- 2 tablespoons almond butter
- 1 tablespoon coconut butter
- ¼ teaspoon almond extract
- 1 teaspoon cacao nibs

Instructions:
1. Add almond milk, banana, dates, almond butter, coconut butter, and almond extract to a blender and blend until smooth.
2. Pour into two glasses, and top with cacao nibs.

3. Enjoy!

Nutrition information:
Calories: 252 kcal, Carbohydrates: 36 g, Protein: 6 g, Fat: 12 g, Sodium: 127 mg, Fiber: 5 g, Sugar: 26 g

32. Watermelon Berry Ninja Smoothie

Welcome to the Watermelon Berry Ninja Smoothie, a delightful and refreshing way to quench your thirst and give you a boost of energy! This smoothie combines the sweetness of watermelon with the tartness of berries, making for an exciting and balanced flavor.
Serving: 1
Preparation Time: 5 minutes
Ready Time: 5 minutes

Ingredients:
- 1 cup diced watermelon
- 1/2 cup frozen blueberries
- 1/2 cup frozen raspberries
- 1/2 cup frozen strawberries
- 1 banana, sliced
- 1/2 cup almond milk

Instructions:
1. Place the diced watermelon, berries, banana, and almond milk in a blender.
2. Blend until the smoothie is thick and creamy.
3. Serve immediately. Enjoy!

Nutrition information:
Calories: 149; Total Fat: 1.6g; Saturated Fat: 0.2g; Cholesterol: 0mg; Sodium: 36mg; Total Carbohydrate: 33.9g; Dietary Fiber: 5.2g; Sugars: 24.7g; Protein: 2.2g.

33. Spinach Mango Coconut Ninja Smoothie

Refreshing and delicious, this creamy Spinach Mango Coconut Ninja Smoothie is packed with antioxidants and vitamins to keep your energy levels up and plenty of fiber to keep you full until your next meal.
Serving: 1
Preparation Time: 5 minutes
Ready Time: 5 minutes

Ingredients:
- 2 cups spinach
- 1 cup frozen mango
- 1/2 cup coconut milk
- 1/2 frozen banana
- 1 teaspoon honey
- 1/2 teaspoon ground ginger
- 1 tablespoon chia seeds

Instructions:
1. Place the spinach, mango, coconut milk, banana, honey, ginger, and chia seeds in a blender and blend until smooth.
2. Serve immediately or store in the refrigerator for later.

Nutrition information:
Calories: 300 kcal
Carbohydrates: 39 g
Fat: 9 g
Protein: 8 g
Fiber: 10 g
Sugar: 22 g

34. Raspberry Coconut Ninja Smoothie

Enjoy a fresh and delicious breakfast with this delicious Raspberry Coconut Ninja Smoothie. This smoothie is vegan, gluten free, dairy free and perfect for a quick and nutritious breakfast.
Serving: 2
Preparation time: 10 minutes
Ready time: 10 minutes

Ingredients:
- 1 cup frozen raspberries
- ½ cup coconut milk
- ¼ cup coconut yogurt
- ¼ cup pineapple chunks
- 2 tablespoons hemp seeds
- 2 tablespoons chia seeds
- 2 tablespoons flaxseed meal
- 1 teaspoon ground cinnamon

Instructions:
1. Combine all Ingredients in a blender and blend until smooth.
2. Divide the smoothie between two glasses and enjoy!

Nutrition information:
Calories: 194 kcal, Carbohydrates: 19.1 g, Protein: 6.5 g, Fat 8.8 g, Cholesterol 0 mg, Sodium 9.5 mg, Fiber 8.2 g, Sugar 8.5 g.

35. Carrot Ginger Ninja Smoothie

This smoothie is the perfect blend of healthy eating and tasty refreshment. With natural and nourishing Ingredients, it provides the perfect balance of sweet and savory.
Serving: Serves 2
Preparation time: 5 minutes
Ready time: 5 minutes

Ingredients:
-2 cups fresh carrot juice
-1 tablespoon minced ginger
-2 tablespoons honey
-1 cup ice cubes

Instructions:
1. In a blender, combine carrot juice, ginger, honey, and ice cubes.
2. Process on high until smooth.
3. Serve immediately.

Nutrition information: Total calories: 160, Protei Carbohydrates: 40g, Sodium: 80mg.

36. Mixed Berry Spinach Ninja Smoo

This Mixed Berry Spinach Ninja Smoothie combines some of the best superfoods to make a colorful, tasty and extremely nourishing smoothie.
Serving: 2
Preparation time: 5 minutes
Ready time: 5 minutes

Ingredients:
- 2 cups fresh spinach
- ½ cup frozen blueberries
- ½ cup frozen strawberries
- ½ cup coconut milk
- 2 tablespoons chia seeds
- 2 tablespoons honey

Instructions:
1. Add the spinach, blueberries, strawberries, coconut milk, chia seeds and honey into a blender.
2. Blend the Ingredients until you reach your desired consistency.
3. Serve.

Nutrition information:
- Calories: 255
- Fat: 6.6g
- Carbohydrates: 50.4g
- Protein: 5.8g
- Vitamin A: 129%
- Vitamin C: 112%
- Calcium: 17%
- Iron: 17%

37. Green Tea Matcha Ninja Smoothie

...is Green Tea Matcha Ninja Smoothie is a delicious and nutritious smoothie filled with matcha green tea and blended with fresh fruits and nuts. It makes for a perfectly energizing start to your day!
Serving: 1
Preparation time: 5 minutes
Ready time: 10 minutes

Ingredients:
- 1½ cup almond milk (or other non-dairy milk)
- 2 teaspoons matcha green tea powder
- 1 frozen banana
- 1 tablespoon almond butter
- 1 handful of fresh spinach
- 1 teaspoon of honey

Instructions:
1. Place almond milk, matcha green tea powder, banana, almond butter, spinach, and honey into a blender.
2. Blend until smooth.
3. Pour into a glass and enjoy!

Nutrition information: This Green Tea Matcha Ninja Smoothie contains:
Calories: 280 kcal
Fat: 12g
Carbohydrates: 33g
Protein: 8g

38. Pineapple Orange Ninja Smoothie

Tired of the same old smoothies? Make yourself the Pineapple Orange Ninja Smoothie and get a burst of flavor plus an added dose of energy! This smoothie is a refreshing blend of pineapple, oranges, and yogurt that creates a delicious treat.
Serving: 2
Preparation Time: 5 minutes
Ready Time: 5 minutes

Ingredients:
- 1/2 cup Greek yogurt
- 1/2 cup frozen pineapple chunks
- 1/2 cup freshly squeezed orange juice
- 2 tablespoons honey

Instructions:
1. In a blender, combine all Ingredients.
2. Blend until all Ingredients are well-combined.
3. Pour into glasses and enjoy!

Nutrition information:
Per serving: Calories: 170, Protein: 10g, Fat: 1.5g, Sodium: 40mg, Carbohydrates: 28.1g, Dietary Fiber: 1.7g

39. Blueberry Peach Ninja Smoothie

A delicious smoothie made with blueberries, peaches, and a few other Ingredients that pack a superfood punch! Perfect for a refreshing breakfast or snack.
Serving: 2
Preparation time: 5 minutes
Ready time: 5 minutes

Ingredients:
- 1 banana
- 1/2 cup fresh or frozen blueberries
- 1/2 cup frozen peaches
- 1/4 cup almond milk or other non-dairy milk
- 2 tablespoons hemp seed hearts
- 1 tablespoon chia seeds
- 1 teaspoon maca powder
- 1 teaspoon spirulina

Instructions:
1. Place banana, blueberries, peaches, almond milk, hemp seed hearts, chia Seeds, maca powder, and spirulina in a blender.
2. Blend until smooth.

3. Serve and enjoy!

Nutrition information: Each serving contains approximately 175 calories, 5 grams of fat, 8 grams of protein, 28 grams of carbohydrates, and 5 grams of fiber.

40. Kiwi Pineapple Spinach Ninja Smoothie

Spark up your day with this smooth and delicious Kiwi Pineapple Spinach Ninja Smoothie! A healthy way to start the day with a burst of flavor.
Serving: 1
Preparation time: 5 minutes
Ready time: 5 minutes

Ingredients:
- 2 cups spinach, tightly packed
- 1 cup pineapple chunks
- 1 kiwi, peeled
- 1 cup unsweetened almond milk
- 1 tablespoon honey

Instructions:
1. Place the spinach, pineapple, kiwi, almond milk, and honey in a blender.
2. Blend until smooth.
3. Serve and enjoy!

Nutrition information: 250 calories, 5g fat, 45g carbohydrates, 4g protein

41. Chocolate Cherry Ninja Smoothie

Enjoy a refreshing twist on your favorite smoothie with this tasty Chocolate Cherry Ninja Smoothie. This smoothie is an all-natural and healthy way to satisfy your sweet tooth without compromising your diet.
Serving: 2

Preparation time: 5 minutes
Ready time: 5 minutes

Ingredients:
-3/4 cup frozen dark tart cherries
-1/2 avocado, pitted
-3/4 cup vanilla almond milk
-2 tablespoons cocoa powder
-1 tablespoon honey or maple syrup
-1/2 teaspoon vanilla extract
- 2 frozen banana

Instructions:
1. Place all Ingredients in a high-powered blender, such as a Ninja blender.
2. Turn blender on and blend until smooth, about a minute.
3. Divide smoothies between two glasses and enjoy immediately.

Nutrition information: Calories: 350; Fat: 8 g; Protein: 6 g; carbohydrates: 69 g; Sodium: 50 mg; Potassium: 1060 mg; Vitamin A: 5 % DV, Vitamin C: 10 % DV; Calcium: 35 % DV; Iron: 4 % DV

42. Mango Banana Coconut Ninja Smoothie

This delicious mango, banana and coconut ninja smoothie, is a great way to start your day. Filled with fresh flavors and creamy goodness, it's a perfect pick-me-up that packs a powerful nutritional punch.
Serving: 2
Preparation Time: 5 minutes
Ready time: 5 minutes

Ingredients:
- 2 cups of frozen mango chunks
- 1 large banana, frozen
- 1/4 cup of coconut milk
- 2 tablespoons of honey
- 1 teaspoon of fresh lemon juice

Instructions:
1. In a blender, combine the frozen mango, banana, coconut milk, honey and lemon juice.
2. Blend until smooth.
3. Serve in a glass or bowl, topped with extra mango chunks and a sprinkle of shredded coconut, if desired.

Nutrition information:
- Calories: 250
- Carbohydrates: 56g
- Protein: 2g
- Fat: 4g
- Sodium: 16mg

43. Strawberry Watermelon Ninja Smoothie

This delicious Strawberry Watermelon Ninja Smoothie is a great way to start your day with! It's packed with fresh and succulent fruits in an easy to make drink.
Serving: 2 small glasses or 1 large glass
Preparation Time: 5 minutes
Ready Time: 5 minutes

Ingredients:
- ½ cup of diced watermelon
- ½ cup of diced strawberries
- ¼ cup of Greek yogurt
- ¼ cup of orange juice
- ½ teaspoon of honey
- A handful of ice cubes

Instructions:
1. Add all the Ingredients into a Ninja blender.
2. Blend until the mixture is smooth and all the Ingredients are combined.
3. Serve immediately in a tall glass. Enjoy!

Nutrition information: 1 serving of Strawberry Watermelon Ninja Smoothie contains approximately 150 calories, 12g of sugar, 2g of fat, and 6g of protein.

44. Cucumber Avocado Ninja Smoothie

Start your day with a healthy, protein-packed Cucumber Avocado Ninja Smoothie! This energizing and delicious smoothie will have you feeling ready to tackle the day.
Serving: 2
Preparation Time: 5 minutes
Ready Time: 5 minutes

Ingredients:
-1 cucumber, peeled and quartered
-1 avocado, peeled, pitted and cubed
-1 cup Greek yogurt
-1 cup almond milk
-1 teaspoon honey
-2 cups spinach
-2 tablespoons chia seeds
-Ice

Instructions:
1. Place cucumber, avocado, yogurt, almond milk, honey, spinach, chia seeds, and ice in a blender.
2. Blend on high for 2-3 minutes, or until mixture is smooth.
3. Serve in 2 glasses and enjoy!

Nutrition information:
Calories: 242, Total Fat: 9.1g, Sodium: 64mg, Potassium: 540mg, Total Carbohydrate: 18.3g, Dietary Fiber: 7.3g, Sugars: 5.7g, Protein: 19.2g

45. Peanut Butter Banana Protein Ninja Smoothie

Peanut Butter Banana Protein Ninja Smoothie is an easy and healthy smoothie that is packed with proteins and natural sweetness. It is a great way to get energized and fueled up on a hectic morning or a busy day.
Serving: 1 large glass
Preparation time: 4 mins
Ready time: 4 mins

Ingredients:
- 1 Banana
- 2 tablespoons Peanut Butter
- 1 cup Milk
- 2 tablespoons Protein Powder
- 2 tablespoons Chia Seeds

Instructions:
1. Peel and slice banana.
2. Place banana slices, peanut butter, milk, protein powder and chia seeds in a blender.
3. Blend on high until smooth.
4. Serve with additional toppings if desired.

Nutrition information:
Calories: 198 kcal
Carbohydrates: 15 g
Protein: 14 g
Fat: 12 g
Sugar: 6 g

46. Orange Raspberry Ninja Smoothie

This Orange Raspberry Ninja Smoothie is a delicious and refreshing way to kickstart your day.
Serving: 1
Preparation Time: 5 minutes
Ready Time: 5 minutes

Ingredients:
- ½ cup fresh or frozen raspberries

- 1 cup freshly squeezed orange juice
- ¼ cup plain Greek yogurt
- 1 tablespoon honey
- 2 tablespoons chia seeds
- 2-3 large ice cubes

Instructions:
1. In a blender, combine the raspberries, orange juice, yogurt, honey, and chia seeds.
2. Blend until well combined and smooth.
3. Add the ice cubes and blend for an additional 5 seconds or until desired consistency is achieved.
4. Serve immediately and enjoy!

Nutrition information:
Calories: 248, Protein: 8g, Total Fat: 5g, Total Carbohydrates: 43g, Fiber: 7g, Sugar: 27g

47. Spinach Pineapple Ninja Smoothie

This Spinach Pineapple Ninja Smoothie packs a powerful combination of flavors with the sweetness of pineapple to make this a nutritious and delicious breakfast drink.
Serving: 4
Preparation time: 5 minutes
Ready time: 5 minutes

Ingredients:
- 2 cups spinach, chopped
- 1 cup fresh or frozen pineapple
- ½ cup plain Greek yogurt
- ¼ cup almond milk
- 2 teaspoons honey
- 1 teaspoon ground flaxseed
- 1 teaspoon chia seeds

Instructions:

1. Place spinach, pineapple, Greek yogurt, almond milk, honey, flaxseed and chia seeds in a blender and blend until completely smooth.
2. Divide the smoothie among 4 glasses and serve.

Nutrition information: Each smoothie provides approximately 165 calories, 10g proteins, 22g carbohydrates, 5g fat, 5g fibre and 18g sugars.

48. Raspberry Mango Ninja Smoothie

Indulge in this delicious raspberry mango ninja smoothie that's packed with nutrients and energy.
Serving: 4
Preparation time: 10 minutes
Ready time: 10 minutes

Ingredients:
- 2 cups of frozen mango
- 2 frozen bananas
- 1 cup of frozen raspberries
- 2 cups of unsweetened almond milk
- 2 tablespoons of honey

Instructions:
1. Place the frozen mango, bananas, and raspberries into a blender.
2. Pour the almond milk and honey into the blender and blend until the mixture reaches a smooth consistency.
3. Divide the raspberry mango smoothie into four glasses.
4. Serve and enjoy!

Nutrition information:
- Calories: 136
- Fat: 2.1g
- Carbohydrates: 33.3g
- Protein: 1.5g

49. Carrot Apple Ginger Ninja Smoothie

Delicious, nutritious, and great tasting, the Carrot Apple Ginger Ninja Smoothie is an innovative and healthy smoothie idea. Featuring a blend of carrots, apples, and ginger, this smoothie is packed with vitamins and other nutrients.
Serving: Makes 1 Serving: Preparation time: 5 minutes or less
Ready time: 5 minutes

Ingredients:
- ½ cup fresh carrot juice
- ½ cup peeled and chopped apple
- ½ teaspoon freshly grated ginger
- ½ teaspoon honey
- ¼ cup ice

Instructions:
1. In a high-speed blender, combine the carrot juice, chopped apple, grated ginger, honey and ice.
2. Blend on high until the mixture is smooth and creamy.
3. Pour the smoothie into a glass and enjoy!

Nutrition information (per serving):
- Calories: 100
- Total Fat: 0g
- Saturated Fat: 0g
- Sodium: 10mg
- Carbohydrates: 25g
- Fiber: 3g
- Sugar: 16g
- Protein: 1g

50. Mixed Berry Greek Yogurt Ninja Smoothie

A delicious and energizing smoothie that can be ready in no time with the power of the Ninja blender. Featuring Greek yogurt and mixed berries, it's a healthy and nutritious snack!
Serving: Makes 2 servings

Preparation Time: 5 minutes
Ready Time: 5 minutes

Ingredients:
- ½ cup Greek yogurt
- ¼ cup mixed berries (fresh or frozen)
- ½ teaspoon honey
- 2 tablespoons ground flaxseed
- 1 cup almond milk

Instructions:
1. Place all Ingredients in a Ninja blender.
2. Blend until smooth.
3. Serve and enjoy!

Nutrition information:
Per Serving: Total Calories 151, Total Fat 5.9g, Saturated Fat 1.1g, Cholesterol 5.3mg, Sodium 70.8mg, Total Carbohydrate 14.7g, Dietary Fiber 2.5g, Total Sugars 9.5g, Protein 8.9g.

51. Green Goddess Ninja Smoothie

Packed with nutrients and bursting with flavor, the Green Goddess Ninja Smoothie is a refreshing and nutritious addition to any breakfast or snack routine.
Serving: 1
Preparation Time: 5 minutes
Ready Time: 5 minutes

Ingredients:
- ½ cup baby spinach
- ½ banana
- ½ avocado
- 1 cup unsweetened almond milk
- 1 scoop of protein powder (optional)
- 1 teaspoon honey or maple syrup (optional)
- Ice

Instructions:
1. Place the spinach, banana, avocado, almond milk, and protein powder in a blender.
2. Blend until smooth.
3. Add honey or maple syrup if desired.
4. Add ice, if desired, to thicken the smoothie.
5. Enjoy!

Nutrition information:
Calories: 214, Fat: 11.7g, Protein: 7.6g, Carbs: 23.7g, Sugar: 10.2g, Fiber: 6.5g, Sodium: 73.4mg

52. Pineapple Banana Ninja Smoothie

Pineapple Banana Ninja Smoothie is a nutritious and delicious treat great for breakfast, snacks, or as a post-workout refresher.
Serving: Makes 2 small smoothies
Preparation time: 5 minutes
Ready time: 5 minutes

Ingredients:
- 1/2 cup chopped pineapple
- 1/2 banana
- 1/2 cup ice cubes
- 1/2 cup yogurt
- 1 tablespoon honey
- 1/2 teaspoon turmeric

Instructions:
1. In a blender, combine pineapple, banana, ice cubes, yogurt, honey and turmeric.
2. Blend for 1 minute.
3. Stop and stir if necessary.
4. Blend until desired texture is reached.
5. Divide the smoothies into 2 glasses and serve.

Nutrition information: Serving size: 1 smoothie. Calories: 115 kcal. Fat: 1 g. Protein: 4 g. Carbs: 24 g. Fiber: 1 g. Sugar: 18 g. Sodium: 66 mg. Potassium 287 mg. Calcium: 179 mg. Iron: 0.9 mg

53. Blueberry Pomegranate Ninja Smoothie

This refreshing Blueberry Pomegranate Ninja Smoothie is a delicious way to start your morning and fuel up for the day ahead.
Serving: Makes 5 cups
Preparation time: 10 minutes
Ready time: 10 minutes

Ingredients:
- 1 cup fresh or frozen wild blueberries
- 1 cup fresh or frozen raspberries
- 2 pomegranates, peeled and seeds removed
- 1 large banana
- 2 tablespoons honey
- 2 cups plain Greek yogurt
- 2 cups unsweetened almond milk

Instructions:
1. Add all the Ingredients into a blender and blend until smooth.
2. Divide smoothie into 5 cups. Serve immediately and enjoy.

Nutrition information: Calories: 150 Total Fat: 2 g Saturated Fat: 0 g Trans Fat: 0 g Cholesterol: 1 mg Sodium: 22 mg Carbohydrates: 32 g Fiber: 9 g Sugar: 16 g Protein: 4 g

54. Kiwi Berry Ninja Smoothie

Kiwi Berry Ninja Smoothie is a colorful and nutrient-dense smoothie made with superfood kiwis and berries.
Serving: 2
Preparation Time: 10 minutes
Ready Time: 10 minutes

Ingredients:
- 2 kiwis, peeled and sliced
- ½ cup frozen raspberry
- ½ cup frozen blueberry
- 2 teaspoons honey
- 2 tablespoons freshly squeezed lemon juice
- 2 cups of cold water

Instructions:
1. Combine peeled and sliced kiwi, frozen raspberry, frozen blueberry, honey, and freshly squeezed lemon juice in a blender.
2. Blend until smooth.
3. Add cold water and blend for an extra minute.
4. Serve the smoothie in glasses and enjoy.

Nutrition information: Per serving (2 servings): Calories: 130, Total Fat: 0.5 g, Sodium: 9 mg, Potassium: 347 mg, Total Carbohydrates: 30 g, Dietary Fiber: 5 g, Sugars: 23 g, Protein: 2 g.

55. Chocolate Mint Ninja Smoothie

This Chocolate Mint Ninja Smoothie is sweet, creamy and bursting with minty goodness. It's like a milkshake in a glass and a great way to start your day.
Serving: 2
Preparation Time: 10 mins
Ready Time: 10 mins

Ingredients:
- 1 ½ cups almond milk
- 2 ½ tablespoons cocoa powder
- 2 tablespoons natural sugar
- ¼ teaspoon pure mint extract
- 2-3 drops green food coloring

Instructions:
1. In a blender, combine almond milk, cocoa powder, sugar and pure mint extract. Blend until smooth.

2. Pour in the smoothie mixture into glasses and add a couple drops of food coloring in each glass.
3. Gently stir the food color into the smoothies until evenly combined.
4. Serve and enjoy!

Nutrition information:
Servings: 2 | Calories: 126 kcal | Carbohydrates: 24 g | Protein: 4 g | Fat: 2 g | Saturated Fat: 1 g | Cholesterol: 0 mg | Sodium: 25 mg | Potassium: 306 mg | Fiber: 4 g | Sugar: 16 g | Vitamin A: 22 IU | Calcium: 286 mg | Iron: 1 mg

56. Watermelon Berry Mint Ninja Smoothie

This tasty Watermelon Berry Mint Ninja Smoothie is perfect for a summertime refreshment. This cool, creamy smoothie is full of fresh fruits and mint and gives a burst of natural sweetness to your day.
Serving: 1 - 2
Preparation time: 5 minutes
Ready time: 5 minutes

Ingredients:
- 2 cups chosen forment cooled watermelon
- 1/2 cup fresh blueberries
- 1/4 cup fresh mint
- 1/4 cup coconut milk
- 1 teaspoon honey (optional)

Instructions:
1. Place the cooled watermelon and blueberries in a blender and blend until smooth.
2. Add in the fresh mint leaves, coconut milk, and honey (optional). Blend until everything is combined and desired texture is reached.
3. Pour into a glass and serve. Enjoy!

Nutrition information:
- Calories: 131
- Total Fat: 4g
- Saturated Fat: 2g

- Sodium: 31mg
- Carbohydrates: 21g
- Fiber: 3g
- Sugar: 15g
- Protein: 2g

57. Mango Spinach Coconut Ninja Smoothie

Start your day with a delicious and nutrient-packed smoothie that tastes as good as it looks. This Mango Spinach Coconut Ninja Smoothie is bursting with flavor and nutrition, making it the perfect healthy breakfast or snack.

Serving: 1
Preparation Time: 10 minutes
Ready Time: 10 minutes

Ingredients:
- 1/2 cup fresh spinach
- 1 cup frozen mango
- 1/2 banana
- 1/2 cup coconut water
- 2 teaspoons honey

Instructions:
1. In a blender, blend the spinach, mango, banana, coconut water, and honey until smooth.
2. Pour into a serving glass and enjoy.

Nutrition information:
- Calories: 162
- Total Fat: 1.1 g
- Cholesterol: 0 mg
- Sodium: 8.4 mg
- Total Carbohydrates: 37.4 g
- Sugars: 28.1 g
- Protein: 2.2 g

58. Strawberry Mango Chia Ninja Smoothie

This recipe for Strawberry Mango Chia Ninja Smoothie is full of fruits, chia seeds, and yogurt. The flavor of mango and strawberries along with a touch of Greek yogurt makes this smoothie a delicious treat.
Serving: 2
Preparation Time: 5 minutes
Ready Time: 10 minutes

Ingredients:
- 1 cup frozen strawberries
- 1 banana
- 1 cup frozen mangoes
- 1 cup plain Greek yogurt
- 2 tablespoons chia seeds
- 1 cup of almond milk

Instructions:
1. In a blender, add the frozen strawberries, banana, frozen mangoes, and plain Greek yogurt.
2. Blend the Ingredients until they are thoroughly combined and pureed.
3. Add the chia seeds and blend once more until they are mixed in.
4. Pour the almond milk into the blender and blend until the desired consistency is reached.
5. Serve the Strawberry Mango Chia Ninja smoothie in two glasses.

Nutrition information: Per Serving: Calories: 216; Total Fat: 6g; Cholesterol: 11mg; Sodium: 64mg; Carbs: 36g; Fiber: 8g; Protein: 12g; Sugar: 18g.

59. Cucumber Celery Green Ninja Smoothie

Introducing Cucumber Celery Green Ninja Smoothie, packed with vitamins and minerals from green vegetables and fruits. This delicious vegan smoothie will give you a boost of energy and plenty of nutrition.
Serving: Serves 2
Preparation Time: 5 mins
Ready Time: 10 mins

Ingredients:
- 2 Cucumbers
- 2 Celery Stalks
- ½ Avocado
- 2 Bananas
- 2 Handfuls of Spinach
- 2 cups of Coconut Water
- ½ cup of Pure Almond Milk

Instructions:
1. Peel and chop cucumbers into quarters. Slice celery into thin slices.
2. Peel and slice avocado. Peel bananas and cut into slices.
3. Place cucumbers, celery, avocado, bananas and spinach into a blender.
4. Add coconut water and almond milk and blend until smooth.
5. Pour into glasses and enjoy!

Nutrition information (per serving):
Calories: 140 kcal;
Protein: 1.5 g;
Fat: 6 g;
Carbohydrates: 16.5 g;
Sugars: 10 g;
Fiber: 5.5 g;
Sodium: 94 mg.

60. Peanut Butter Chocolate Protein Ninja Smoothie

Start your day (or refuel after a workout) with this delicious and nutrition-rich Peanut Butter Chocolate Protein Ninja Smoothie. Made with a mix of natural peanut butter, almond milk, banana, and protein powder, it's an energizing and filling breakfast or snack option.
Serving: 1
Preparation Time: 5 minutes
Ready Time: 5 minutes

Ingredients:
- 2 tablespoons of natural peanut butter

- 1 banana, frozen
- 1 scoop of protein powder
- 1 cup of unsweetened almond milk

Instructions:
1. Place all Ingredients into a blender.
2. Blend until smooth.
3. Pour into a glass. Enjoy!

Nutrition information:
Calories: 350
Fat: 15 g
Carbohydrates: 23 g
Protein: 31 g

61. Orange Pineapple Ginger Ninja Smoothie

Get ready to be blown away by this tangy, sweet and spicy Orange Pineapple Ginger Ninja Smoothie. With only five simple Ingredients this smoothie will bring the most intense combination of flavors.
Serving: Makes 2 servings
Preparation Time: 5 minutes
Ready Time: 5 minutes

Ingredients:
- 2 cups freshly squeezed orange juice
- 1 cup fresh pineapple chunks
- ½ teaspoon freshly grated ginger
- 1 teaspoon sugar (optional)
- 2-3 ice cubes

Instructions:
1. Place orange juice, pineapple chunks, and ginger in a blender.
2. Blend until smooth.
3. Add sugar, if desired, and blend for a few more seconds.
4. Add ice cubes and blend again until desired texture is achieved.
5. Divide content between two glasses and serve.

Nutrition information:
Per Serving - 121 calories, 0 g fat, 31 g carbohydrate, 1 g protein, 10 mg sodium, 0 g dietary fibre.

62. Spinach Blueberry Ninja Smoothie

Ready to up your smoothie game? This Spinach Blueberry Ninja Smoothie is a wholesome, antioxidant-rich treat that also packs a protein punch.
Serving: Serves 1
Preparation time: 5 minutes
Ready Time: 5 minutes

Ingredients:
- 1 scoop vanilla protein powder
- 1 cup spinach
- ½ cup blueberries
- 1 banana
- ½ cup Greek yogurt
- 1 cup almond milk

Instructions:
1. Add all Ingredients to a blender.
2. Blend until smooth.
3. Serve and enjoy!

Nutrition information: Per serving: Calories 343, Total Fat 6g, Sat. Fat 1g, Sodium 242mg, Total Carbs 37g, Sugars 22g, Protein 30g

63. Raspberry Peach Ninja Smoothie

This Raspberry Peach Ninja Smoothie is a delicious and refreshing way to get your day started. You can also make it as a snack. It's a great way to get some vitamins and fiber, and the sweetness of the peaches and raspberries give it a delicious flavor.
Serving: Makes 4 servings.
Preparation time:

5 minutes.
Ready time: 10 minutes.

Ingredients:
- 2 cups frozen peaches
- 2 small oranges, peeled
- ½ cup frozen raspberries
- 1-2 cups orange juice
- 1 tablespoon honey
- Optional: 1 teaspoon chia seeds, 1 teaspoon flax seeds

Instructions:
1. In a blender or food processor, add the peaches, oranges, raspberries, orange juice, and honey. Blend until smooth.
2. Divide the smoothie into four glasses.
3. Top with chia seeds or flax seeds, if desired.
4. Serve and enjoy.

Nutrition information:
Per serving: 140 kcal, 0.7 g fat, 32 g carbohydrate, 4.3 g dietary fiber, 2.4 g protein.

64. Carrot Orange Ninja Smoothie

Start your day with a ninja-worthy smoothie. Carrot Orange Ninja Smoothie is a delicious and nutritious combination of flavours that will be sure to delight and energize you for hours.
Serving: 1
Preparation Time: 5 minutes
Ready Time: 5 minutes

Ingredients:
- ½ cup cold pressed orange juice
- 1 medium carrot, peeled and roughly chopped
- ½ frozen banana
- ¼ teaspoon ground cinnamon
- 1 teaspoon honey

Instructions:
1. Place the orange juice, carrot, banana, cinnamon, and honey in a blender and blend until smooth.
2. Serve in a glass and enjoy!

Nutrition information:
Calories: 143, Carbohydrates: 33g, Protein: 1g, Fat: 0.3g, Sodium: 16mg, Sugar: 20g.

65. Mixed Berry Oatmeal Ninja Smoothie

This easy and delicious Mixed Berry Oatmeal Ninja Smoothie is the perfect way to start your day. Packed with antioxidant-rich berries, fiber-filled oatmeal, and protein-rich Greek yogurt, this smoothie is loaded with essential vitamins and minerals.
Serving: Makes 1 smoothie
Preparation Time: 5 minutes
Ready Time: 5 minutes

Ingredients:
- ½ cup frozen mixed berries
- ⅓ cup rolled oats
- ⅓ cup plain Greek yogurt
- ½ cup unsweetened almond milk
- ½ teaspoon vanilla extract
- Ice, to taste

Instructions:
1. Add all the Ingredients to a blender and blend until smooth and creamy.
2. Pour the smoothie into a cup and enjoy!

Nutrition information:
- Calories: 293
- Total Fat: 5.8g
- Sodium: 162mg
- Total Carbs: 46g
- Dietary Fiber: 5.6g

- Sugars: 9.7g
- Protein: 11.6g

66. Green Avocado Ninja Smoothie

Jump-start your day with this healthy Green Avocado Ninja Smoothie! Quick and easy to make, this smoothie is packed with nutrition and deliciousness.
Serving: 2-3
Preparation time: 5 minutes
Ready time: 5 minutes

Ingredients:
- ½ ripe avocado
- 1 cup light coconut milk
- 2 tablespoons of chia seeds
- 2-3 tablespoons of raw honey
- 2 cups packed fresh baby spinach
- 1 banana
- Ice cubes

Instructions:
1. Place all the Ingredients into a blender and blend until smooth.
2. Pour into a glass and enjoy immediately.

Nutrition information:
Calories: 390 | Protein: 8.4g | Fat: 16.9g | Carbs: 63.3g | Sodium: 46.2mg | Fiber: 14.2g

67. Pineapple Coconut Lime Ninja Smoothie

This delicious Pineapple Coconut Lime Ninja Smoothie is the perfect way to start your day with a refreshing and healthy blend of flavors. It's tart, tangy, sweet, and easy to make.
Serving: Makes 1-2 servings
Preparation time: 5 minutes
Ready time: 5 minutes

Ingredients:
- 1 cup diced pineapple
- ½ cup coconut milk
- ½ cup ice cubes
- Juice of ½ lime
- 1 teaspoon agave or honey
- Lemon or lime wedges for garnish (optional)

Instructions:
1. Place the pineapple, coconut milk, ice cubes, lime juice, and agave or honey in a blender.
2. Blend until the Ingredients are combined and smooth.
3. Pour the smoothie into two glasses and add a lime or lemon wedge for a garnish (optional).

Nutrition information:
Calories: 140 calories; Fat: 6 g; Cholesterol: 0 g; Sodium: 10 mg; Carbohydrates: 19.5 g; Sugar: 16 g; Protein: 1 g.

68. Blueberry Banana Ninja Smoothie

This delicious and nutritious Blueberry Banana Ninja Smoothie is the perfect snack or breakfast. It's packed with fresh fruit, yogurt, and chia seeds for added fiber and protein. It's quick and easy to make, and can be whipped up in no time.
Serving: 1
Preparation time: 5 minutes
Ready time: 5 minutes

Ingredients:
- 1 banana
- 1 cup frozen blueberries
- ½ cup plain Greek yogurt (or dairy-free variety)
- ¼ cup almond or coconut milk
- 1 tablespoon chia seeds
- 1 teaspoon honey or maple syrup (optional)

Instructions:
1. In a blender, combine the banana, blueberries, yogurt, milk, chia seeds, and honey (if using) and blend until smooth.
2. Serve and enjoy!

Nutrition information
- Calories: 330
- Carbohydrates: 56g
- Protein: 10g
- Fiber: 7g
- Fat: 9g

69. Kiwi Green Apple Ninja Smoothie

Our Kiwi Green Apple Ninja Smoothie is packed with nutrition and is the perfect snack for your active lifestyle. It is an energizing and refreshing smoothie with the perfect balance of flavor.
Serving: 2-3
Prep Time: 10 minutes
Ready Time: 10 minutes

Ingredients:
- 2 kiwis, peeled and chopped
- 1 green apple, cored and chopped
- 2 cups almond milk
- 2 tablespoons chia seeds
- 1 tablespoon honey
- 1/2 teaspoon ground cinnamon

Instructions:
1. Place the kiwis and apple pieces in a blender and blend until smooth.
2. Add the almond milk, chia seeds, honey, and cinnamon. Blend until combined.
3. Serve immediately or transfer to an air-tight container and store in the refrigerator.

Nutrition information: per serving – Calories: 228, Fat: 4g, Carbohydrates: 46g, Protein: 6g

70. Chocolate Hazelnut Ninja Smoothie

This chocolate hazelnut ninja smoothie is packed with goodness. Enjoy the delicious and creamy combination of chocolate and hazelnut for a nutritious, healthy breakfast cereal, snack, or post-workout treat.
Serving: 2
Preparation Time: 5 minutes
Ready Time: 5 minutes

Ingredients:
- 1/3 cup of Dutch process cocoa powder
- 1/2 cup of hazelnut butter
- 1/2 cup of almond milk
- 1/2 cup of Greek yogurt
- 1 banana
- 2 tablespoons of honey
- 1/4 teaspoon of vanilla extract

Instructions:
1. In a blender, combine cocoa powder, hazelnut butter, almond milk, Greek yogurt, banana, honey, and vanilla extract.
2. Blend until all Ingredients are blended and the mixture is smooth.
3. Serve smoothie in two glasses and enjoy your chocolate hazelnut ninja smoothie!

Nutrition information:
Calories: 375
Carbohydrates: 45g
Fat: 18g
Protein: 10g
Sugar: 29g
Fiber: 5g

71. Watermelon Mint Lime Ninja Smoothie

Beat the summer heat with this refreshing and flavorful Watermelon Mint Lime Ninja Smoothie! The sweet and tart combo of watermelon, lime, and mint makes it a refreshing beverage, without added sugar.
Serving: 2
Preparation time: 5 minutes
Ready time: 5 minutes

Ingredients:
- 2 cups of cold watermelon cubes
- Juice of 1 lime
- ¼ cup packed fresh mint leaves
- 2-3 ice cubes

Instructions:
1. In a blender, combine the watermelon, lime juice, and mint leaves.
2. Blend on high speed until smooth.
3. Add the ice cubes and continue blending for 30 seconds.
4. Serve the smoothie in two glasses. Enjoy!

Nutrition information: Each serving provides approximately 120 calories, 1 g fat, 0 g saturated fat, 0 mg cholesterol, 29 g carbohydrates, 3 g fiber, 16 g natural sugars, 2 g protein and 20 mg sodium.

72. Mango Banana Spinach Ninja Smoothie

This is a delicious Mango Banana Spinach Ninja Smoothie recipe that's easy to make and full of vitamins and minerals!
Serving: Makes 1-2 small or 1 large Serving: Preparation Time: 10 minutes
Ready Time: 10 minutes

Ingredients:
- 1 ripe, peeled mango
- 1 ripe banana
- 2 handfuls of fresh spinach
- 8-10 ounces of almond or coconut milk
- 2 tablespoons of flax seed

- 2 teaspoons of honey (optional)
- 1 teaspoon of vanilla extract (optional)

Instructions:
1. Place the mango, banana, spinach and almond or coconut milk in a blender.
2. Blend until smooth.
3. Add the flax seed, honey and vanilla extract and blend until combined.
4. Serve in a glass and enjoy!

Nutrition information:
- Calories: 139
- Carbohydrates: 28.4g
- Protein: 3.4g
- Fat: 2.5g
- Sodium: 22.4mg
- Fiber: 4.7g
- Sugar: 15.4g

73. Cherry Almond Ninja Smoothie

This Cherry Almond Ninja Smoothie is an delicious vegan beverage that makes for a great pre or post workout snack.
Serving – 1
Preparation Time – 5 minutes
Ready Time – 5 minutes

Ingredients:
1 banana, frozen; 1/2 cup cherries, frozen; 2 tablespoons almond butter; 1/2 cup almond milk;

Instructions:
1. Place all Ingredients in a blender and blend until smooth.
2. Pour into a cup and enjoy.

Nutrition information – 360 calories; 16g protein; 37g carbohydrates; 16g fat.

74. Green Matcha Ninja Smoothie

This Green Matcha Ninja Smoothie is a delicious blend of creamy, antioxidant-rich matcha and hearty veggies that are sure to help you get your daily fill of greens! Packed with essential vitamins and minerals, this creamy smoothie is the perfect way to start off your day.
Serving: 1
Preparation Time: 10 minutes
Ready Time: 10 minutes

Ingredients:
- 2 cups spinach
- 1 ripe banana
- 1/2 cup almond milk
- 1 teaspoon matcha green tea powder
- 2 tablespoons protein powder (optional)
- 1/2 teaspoon honey (optional)

Instructions:
1. Add all Ingredients into a blender and blend until smooth.
2. Pour the smoothie into a tall glass or cup and enjoy!

Nutrition information:
Calories: 168, Total Fat: 2g, Saturated Fat: 0g, Cholesterol: 0mg, Sodium: 102mg, Potassium: 605mg, Carbohydrates: 32g, Fiber: 4g, Sugar: 15g, Protein: 8g.

75. Dragon Fruit Berry Ninja Smoothie

Introducing the Dragon Fruit Berry Ninja Smoothie! This smoothie is blast of fruity taste and flavor, perfectly balanced by a hint of nutty vanilla. Not only is it delicious, but it's also incredibly nutritious and loaded with antioxidants to help you maintain good health.
Serving: 1
Preparation Time: 5 minutes
Ready Time: 5 minutes

Ingredients:
- 1/2 dragon fruit, peeled and chopped
- 1/2 cup frozen raspberries
- ½ banana
- ½ cup almond milk
- 1 teaspoon vanilla extract
- 1/2 teaspoon ground almond or peanut butter

Instructions:
1. Place the dragon fruit, raspberries, banana, almond milk, vanilla extract and ground almond/peanut butter in a blender.
2. Blend the Ingredients together on high speed until the Ingredients are smooth and creamy.
3. Pour the smoothie into a tall glass and enjoy.

Nutrition information:
Serving size: 1
Calories: 167
Fat: 6.2g
Carbohydrates: 28g
Protein: 3.3g

76. Peach Mango Ginger Ninja Smoothie

This Peach Mango Ginger Ninja Smoothie is a zesty and incredibly tasty combination of peaches, mangoes, ginger, and the so-called "ninja" Ingredients for an extra boost. It's a great way to start your day and a perfect post-workout beverage.
Serving: 1 glass
Preparation Time: 5 minutes
Ready Time: 5 minutes

Ingredients:
- 1/2 cup frozen peaches
- 1/2 cup frozen mangoes
- ½ tsp freshly grated ginger
- Juice of 2 limes
- 1 banana

- 2 cups of coconut water
- A handful of ice cubes
- Optional: 1 tbsp of raw honey to sweeten (optional)

Instructions:
1. Place all the Ingredients in a high-speed blender.
2. Blend for about one minute or until everything is nicely combined and there are no chunks visible.
3. Taste and adjust sweetness if desired.
4. Pour the smoothie into a glass and serve!

Nutrition information (per glass):
Calories=184, Protein=3g, Total Fat=1g, Sodium=46mg, Total Carb=45g, Dietary Fiber=4g, Sugar=36g

77. Pineapple Spinach Coconut Ninja Smoothie

Enjoy this delicious Pineapple Spinach Coconut Ninja Smoothie, perfect for a post-workout or on the go breakfast.
Serving: 2
Preparation Time: 10 minutes
Ready Time: 10 minutes

Ingredients:
- 2 cups spinach
- 2 cups diced pineapple
- 2 tablespoons shredded coconut
- 1 cup almond milk
- 1 teaspoon honey

Instructions:
1. In a blender, combine spinach, diced pineapple, shredded coconut, almond milk, and honey.
2. Blend until all the Ingredients are fully incorporated.
3. If desired, add additional almond milk for a thinner consistency.
4. Serve chilled.

Nutrition information:

Calories: 148 kcal, Protein: 2.4 g, Carbohydrates: 31.2 g, Fat: 2.7 g, Sodium: 75 mg, Fiber: 3.9 g, Sugar: 24.6 g.

78. Raspberry Coconut Chia Ninja Smoothie

This Raspberry Coconut Chia Ninja Smoothie is a delicious on-the-go breakfast packed with fiber, vitamins, and proteins.
Serving: 1 smoothie
Preparation Time: 5 minutes
Ready Time: 5 minutes

Ingredients:
- ¼ cup frozen raspberries
- ¼ cup coconut yogurt
- ¼ cup unsweetened almond milk
- 1 tablespoon chia seeds
- 1 teaspoon honey (optional)

Instructions:
1. Place all the Ingredients in a blender.
2. Blend for about 1 minute or until the mixture is mostly smooth.
3. Pour the smoothie into a glass, add optional toppings and enjoy!

Nutrition information: Each serving of Raspberry Coconut Chia Ninja Smoothie contains 135 calories, 13 g of carbohydrates, 5 g of fat, 3 g of fiber, 7 g of sugar, and 4 g of protein.

79. Carrot Turmeric Ginger Ninja Smoothie

Carrot Turmeric Ginger Ninja Smoothie is an exotic blend of carrot, turmeric, and ginger that is healthy and scrumptious. This smoothie is perfect for a quick snack or a healthy breakfast.
Serving: 2
Preparation Time: 5 minutes
Ready Time: 10 minutes

Ingredients:

- 2 carrots, peeled and chopped
- ½ teaspoon of turmeric
- 1 tablespoon of grated ginger
- 1 cup of coconut milk
- 2 tablespoons of honey
- 2 tablespoons of yoghurt

Instructions:
1. In a blender, add all the Ingredients – carrots, turmeric, ginger, coconut milk, honey, and yogurt.
2. Blend until smooth and creamy.
3. Pour into two glasses and enjoy!

Nutrition information:
Serving size – 1 glass of Carrot Turmeric Ginger Ninja Smoothie
Calories – 140
Fat – 5g
Protein – 2g
Carbohydrates – 25g

80. Spirulina Blueberry Ninja Smoothie

This Spirulina Blueberry Ninja Smoothie is a healthy, tasty and refreshing way to get your essential antioxidants! Packed full of soothing blueberry goodness, nutritious spirulina, and fresh banana, this smoothie is worth every sip.
Serving:3-4
Preparation Time:10 minutes
Ready Time: 10 minutes

Ingredients:
- 1 ripe banana
- 1 cup frozen blueberries
- 1 cup plain yogurt
- 1/2 cup skim milk
- 2 teaspoons spirulina powder

Instructions:

1. In a blender, blend the banana, blueberries, and yogurt until smooth.
2. Slowly add the milk and mix until the consistency is smooth.
3. Add in the spirulina powder and mix until it is fully incorporated.
4. Pour the smoothie into glasses or a mason jar for easy portability.
Enjoy your Spirulina Blueberry Ninja Smoothie!

Nutrition information:
- Calories: 132
- Carbs: 24 g
- Protein: 6 g
- Fat: 0.4 g.

81. Mango Pineapple Ginger Ninja Smoothie

This Mango Pineapple Ginger Ninja Smoothie is a combination of tropical and spicy flavors that together make for an energizing, vitamin-packed drink!
Serving: Makes 2 smoothies
Preparation time: 5 minutes
Ready time: 5 minutes

Ingredients:
- 2 cups frozen mango
- 1 cup pineapple chunks
- 1 inch chunk fresh ginger root
- 1/2 cup non-dairy milk

Instructions:
1. Place all Ingredients in a high-powered blender, then blend until smooth.
2. Pour into two glasses, then enjoy your amazing tropical smoothie!

Nutrition information: Calories 119, Total Fat 1.3 g, Saturated Fat 0.8 g, Cholesterol 0 mg, Sodium 64.5 mg, Total Carbohydrate 25.8 g, Dietary Fiber 3.1 g, Sugar 18.7 g, Protein 2.1 g.

82. Banana Oatmeal Ninja Smoothie

Get your day off to a nourishing and delicious start with a Banana Oatmeal Ninja Smoothie! This simple breakfast smoothie is incredibly healthy, filling and so full of flavor that the whole family will love it.
Serving: 2
Preparation Time: 5 minutes
Ready Time: 5 minutes

Ingredients:
- 1 banana
- 1/2 cup oats
- 1 cup almond milk
- 1/2 teaspoon ground cinnamon
- 1/4 teaspoon ground nutmeg

Instructions:
1. Place banana, oats, almond milk, cinnamon and nutmeg into blender.
2. Blend all of the Ingredients on high until smooth.
3. Pour into two glasses and serve.

Nutrition information: Per serving size: 217 calories, 4g fat, 44g carbohydrates, 7g protein.

83. Mixed Berry Kale Ninja Smoothie

This Mixed Berry Kale Ninja Smoothie is a delicious and nutritious breakfast smoothie that will boost your energy levels and start your day off right! A combination of fresh berries, nutritious kale, and creamy yogurt, this smoothie is a healthy and vitamin-packed treat.
Serving: Serves 4
Preparation time: 5 minutes
Ready time: 5 minutes

Ingredients:
- 1 cup frozen strawberries
- 1 cup frozen raspberries
- 1 banana

- 2 cups kale leaves
- 2 cups plain Greek yogurt
- 1 cup almond or soy milk
- 2 tablespoons honey

Instructions:
1. Add the frozen strawberries, raspberries, banana, kale leaves, yogurt, milk, and honey to a blender.
2. Blend all the Ingredients until the smoothie is smooth and creamy.
3. Divide the smoothie into four glasses and serve immediately.

Nutrition information: Per serving: calories 242, fat 4g, saturated fat 1g, cholesterol 11mg, sodium 77mg, carbohydrates 39g, fiber 6g, protein 16g.

84. Watermelon Cucumber Mint Ninja Smoothie

Meet the Watermelon Cucumber Mint Ninja Smoothie, a delicious and refreshingly healthy smoothie that packs a punch. It is easy to make and perfect for a summer day outside.
Serving: 4
Preparation Time: 5 minutes
Ready Time: 10 minutes

Ingredients:
- 2 cups sliced watermelon
- 2 English cucumbers, peeled
- 1/4 cup fresh mint leaves
- 1/2 cup ice
- 1 cup vanilla coconut milk
- 3 tablespoons honey

Instructions:
1. Combine the watermelon, cucumbers, mint leaves, and ice in a blender.
2. Blend until smooth, scraping down the sides of the blender as needed.
3. Add the coconut milk and honey, blending until combined.
4. Divide the smoothie among 4 glasses and serve immediately.

Nutrition information:
Calories: 227 kcal; Carbohydrates: 51 g; Protein: 2 g; Fat: 4 g; Saturated Fat: 3 g; Cholesterol: 5 mg; Sodium: 50 mg; Potassium: 556 mg; Fiber: 2 g; Sugar: 47 g; Vitamin A: 855 IU; Vitamin C: 24 mg; Calcium: 93 mg; Iron: 1 mg.

85. Cherry Vanilla Almond Ninja Smoothie

This Cherry Vanilla Almond Ninja Smoothie is a fresh, flavorful, and nutritious snack sure to keep you energized all day! It's loaded with cherries, almond butter, vanilla, and almond milk for a creamy, dreamy pick-me-up.
Serving:
Makes 2 servings
Preparation Time:
5 minutes
Ready time:
5 minutes

Ingredients:
- 1 cup frozen pitted cherries
- 2 tablespoons creamy almond butter
- 1/2 teaspoon pure vanilla extract
- 1 cup unsweetened almond milk

Instructions:
1. Put the cherries, almond butter, vanilla, and almond milk into a blender.
2. Blend on high until the mixture is smooth and creamy.
3. Divide the smoothie between two glasses and enjoy!

Nutrition information:
Calories 246, Fat 12g, Sodium 108mg, Carbohydrate 27g, Fiber 5g, Protein 7g

86. Avocado Lime Ninja Smoothie

Bursting with a refreshing blend of creamy avocado and tart lime, this healthy Avocado Lime Ninja Smoothie will quickly become one of your favorite on-the-go drinks!
Serving: 2
Preparation Time: 5 minutes
Ready Time: 5 minutes

Ingredients:
- ½ of an avocado
- ½ cup of almond milk (or any dairy-free milk of your choice)
- ¼ cup of fresh lime juice (or more – depending on how tart you like it)
- 1 teaspoon of honey
- 1 handful of ice

Instructions:
1. Put all the Ingredients into a blender and blend until smooth.
2. Serve right away in two glasses and enjoy!

Nutrition information: Nutritional value per serving: 118 calories; 7 grams fat; 3 grams protein; 13 grams carbohydrates; 4 grams fiber

87. Spinach Mango Banana Ninja Smoothie

This Spinach Mango Banana Ninja smoothie is packed with vitamins, minerals, fiber, and antioxidants and will make you feeling energized and healthy.
Serving: 1
Preparation Time: 5 minutes
Ready Time: 5 minutes

Ingredients:
- 1 cup fresh spinach
- 1/2 cup fresh mango, frozen
- 1/2 banana, frozen
- 1/4 cup plain Greek yogurt
- 1/2 cup unsweetened almond milk

Instructions:
1. Place spinach, mango, banana, Greek yogurt and almond milk in a blender.
2. Blend on high for 1 minute until all Ingredients are incorporated and the smoothie is creamy.
3. Serve immediately.

Nutrition information: (per serving)
Calories: 133
Fat: 0g
Carbohydrates: 25.9g
Protein: 6.5g
Fiber: 3.3g

88. Coconut Berry Ninja Smoothie

This Coconut Berry Ninja Smoothie is a delicious and nutritious way to start off your day! This vegan-friendly smoothie has a smooth, creamy texture and a combination of tart and sweet flavors that make it a refreshing treat.
Serving: Serves 1
Preparation time: 5 minutes
Ready time: 5 minutes

Ingredients:
- ½ cup fresh coconut cream
- ½ cup frozen mixed berries
- 2 tablespoons chia seeds
- 1 banana, frozen
- 1 teaspoon honey or agave syrup
- 1 tablespoon coconut oil
- ½ cup almond milk

Instructions:
1. Place coconut cream, frozen berries and chia seeds in a blender and mix until combined.
2. Add banana, honey, coconut oil and almond milk, blend until smooth.

3. Serve the smoothie in your favourite glass and enjoy!

Nutrition information:
Calories: 400 kcal, Fat: 24.8 g, Carbohydrates: 38.8 g, Protein: 8.4 g, Sodium: 19 mg, Fiber: 9.2 g, Sugar: 18.5 g.

89. Pineapple Orange Ginger Ninja Smoothie

Try this deliciously fresh and simple Pineapple Orange Ginger Ninja Smoothie. A perfect combination of sweetness and spice to start your day off right!
Serving: 1
Preparation time: 5 minutes
Ready Time: 5 minutes

Ingredients:
- 1/2 cup frozen pineapple
- 1/2 cup freshly squeezed orange juice
- 1 tablespoon freshly grated ginger

Instructions:
1. Place the frozen pineapple in a blender and pulse until the pineapple is chopped into small chunks.
2. Add the orange juice and ginger to the blender and blend until everything is well incorporated.
3. Pour the smoothie into a glass and enjoy!

Nutrition information (per serving):
- Calories: 108
- Protein: 1g
- Fat: 0g
- Carbs: 27g

90. Green Kiwi Ninja Smoothie

Cool down and fuel up with this refreshing Green Kiwi Ninja Smoothie! With banana, pineapple, and coconut juice, this smoothie is a great way

to get your daily minerals, healthy fats, and fiber while also giving you a great boost of energy!
Serving: 1
Preparation time: 5 minutes
Ready time: 5 minutes

Ingredients:
- 2 bananas
- 1 cup pineapple
- ½ cup coconut juice
- ½ cup spinach
- 1 kiwi, peeled

Instructions:
1. Add the bananas, pineapple, coconut juice, spinach, and kiwi to a blender.
2. Blend on high for 1-2 minutes until the Ingredients are fully blended together.
3. Pour the smoothie into a glass and enjoy!

Nutrition information:
- Calories: 220
- Protein: 3g
- Carbs: 55g
- Total Fat: 2g
- Fiber: 7g

91. Chocolate Raspberry Ninja Smoothie

This Chocolate Raspberry Ninja Smoothie is made with dairy-free coconut milk, dark chocolate and fresh or frozen raspberries and is the perfect way to start the day!
Serving: Serves 2
Preparation time: 5 minutes
Ready time: 5 minutes

Ingredients:
- 2 cups dairy-free coconut milk

- 1/2 cup dark chocolate chips
- 1/2 cup fresh or frozen raspberries

Instructions:
1. In a blender, combine the dairy-free coconut milk, dark chocolate chips and raspberries.
2. Blend until smooth.
3. Divide between two glasses and serve.

Nutrition information: Per serving (1 glass): 105 Calories, 8 g Fat, 7 g Carbohydrates, 2 g Protein.

92. Strawberry Coconut Ninja Smoothie

This Strawberry Coconut Ninja Smoothie is a delightful and refreshing combination of sweet and tangy flavors. Packed with protein and healthy fats, this smoothie is sure to give you a great start to the day.
Serving: 1
Preparation Time: 5 mins
Ready Time: 5 mins

Ingredients:
- 1 banana
- ½ cup frozen strawberries
- ¼ cup unsweetened coconut flakes
- ¼ cup oats
- 2 tablespoons almond butter
- ¼ cup unsweetened almond milk

Instructions:
1. Place banana, strawberries, coconut flakes, oats, almond butter and almond milk into a blender.
2. Blend until Ingredients are smooth and combined.
3. Serve your Strawberry Coconut Ninja Smoothie in a glass and enjoy.

Nutrition information
Calories: 258 kcal, Carbohydrates: 32 g, Protein: 7 g, Fat: 12 g, Sodium: 52 mg, Fiber: 5 g, Sugar: 15 g

93. Blueberry Acai Ninja Smoothie

Start your day off right with this deliciously refreshing Blueberry Acai Ninja Smoothie! Combining the antioxidants of blueberries and acai berry together, this sip-able dream provides a powerful blast of energy to get you going in the morning.
Serving: 2
Preparation Time: 15 minutes
Ready Time: 15 minutes

Ingredients:
- 1/2 cup frozen blueberries
- 2 frozen ripe bananas
- 2 pitted Medjool dates
- 2 tablespoons raw cacao powder
- 1 teaspoon maca powder
- 1 cup unsweetened almond milk
- 1/2 cup ice
- 2 teaspoons acai berry powder

Instructions:
1. Blend the frozen blueberries, bananas, dates, cacao powder, maca powder, and almond milk into a blender.
2. Blend until fully combined and thickened.
3. Add the ice and acai berry powder, blending until smooth.
4. Serve and enjoy!

Nutrition information: per serving (1 smoothie)
- Calories: 290
- Total Fat: 3.7g
- Total Carbohydrates: 63.6g
- Sugar: 23.4g
- Protein: 2.9g

94. Green Apple Celery Ninja Smoothie

Enjoy a super nutritious and tasty nutrition-packed drink with this Green Apple Celery Ninja Smoothie! You'll be left feeling refreshed and energized.
Serving: 1-2
Preparation Time: 5 minutes
Ready Time: 5 minutes

Ingredients:
- 1/2 cup celery, chopped
- 1/2 cup green apple, chopped
- 1/2 cup frozen pineapple
- 1/2 banana
- 8 ounces vanilla almond milk

Instructions:
1. Place all Ingredients into blender in the order listed.
2. Blend until desired texture is achieved.
3. Serve immediately after blending.

Nutrition information:
Calories: 238 kcal, Carbohydrates: 45 g, Protein: 5 g, Fat: 4 g, Saturated Fat: 1 g, Cholesterol: 0 mg, Sodium: 96 mg, Potassium: 360 mg, Fiber: 7 g, Sugar: 28 g, Vitamin A: 207 IU, Vitamin C: 16 mg, Calcium: 169 mg, Iron: 1 mg

95. Peanut Butter Espresso Ninja Smoothie

A wholesome and nutritiously dense blend, this Peanut Butter Espresso Ninja Smoothie is sure to give you the energy needed to make it through your day.
Serving: 2 portions
Preparation Time: 4 minutes
Ready Time: 4 minutes

Ingredients:
- 1/2 cup cold brewed espresso
- 1/2 cup almond milk or coconut milk
- 1/2 cup organic peanut butter

- 1/2 cup ice
- 1 banana
- 1 scoop protein powder
- Optional toppings: shredded coconut, peanut butter, banana slices

Instructions:
1. Place all Ingredients in a high-speed blender.
2. Blend on high for 1-2 minutes, or until everything is completely blended together and smooth.
3. Divide the smoothie between 2 glasses and add optional toppings.

Nutrition information:
Calories per serving: 522
Total fat: 29 g
Saturated fat: 4.2 g
Cholesterol: 0 mg
Sodium: 215.7 mg
Total Carbohydrates: 38.5 g
Dietary Fiber: 6.2 g
Protein: 20.3 g

96. Orange Turmeric Ninja Smoothie

Start the day off right with this wake-me-up Ninja Smoothie. Curated with a perfect balance of creamy, sweet and tart flavors, this Orange Turmeric Ninja Smoothie is both refreshing and energizing.
Serving: 1
Preparation Time: 5 minutes
Ready Time: 5 minutes

Ingredients:
- ½ cup freshly squeezed orange juice
- ½ cup plain Greek yogurt or almond milk yogurt
- ½ cup frozen mango
- ½ ripe banana
- ½ teaspoon freshly grated turmeric
- 1 tablespoon honey
- Green stevia, to taste (optional)

Instructions:
1. Place all of the Ingredients in a high-speed blender.
2. Blend until smooth.
3. Pour into a glass and enjoy!

Nutrition information (per serving):
- CALORIES: 218 kcal
- PROTEIN: 6 grams
- TOTAL FAT: 2 grams
- TOTAL CARBS: 47 grams
- FIBER: 4 grams
- SUGAR: 30 grams

97. Papaya Lime Mint Ninja Smoothie

This Papaya Lime Mint Ninja Smoothie is a refreshing, citrusy and delicious smoothie perfect for a summer day. The combination of the 3 main fruits makes it unique and irresistible.
Serving: 2
Preparation Time: 10 minutes
Ready Time: 10 minutes

Ingredients:
- ⅔ cup cubed ripe papaya
- ¼ cup freshly squeezed lime juice
- ¼ cup freshly chopped mint leaves
- 1 cup coconut milk
- 1 tablespoon honey (optional)

Instructions:
1. Place the papaya cubes, freshly squeezed lime juice, freshly chopped mint leaves and coconut milk in a blender and blend until smooth.
2. Once done, add the honey and pulse the blender so that the honey is just mixed and not blended.
3. Pour into two glasses and enjoy your smoothie!

Nutrition information:

- Total Calories: 165
- Fat: 9.9 g
- Carbohydrates: 22.8 g
- Protein: 1.7 g

98. Mango Pineapple Coconut Water Ninja Smoothie

Take your smoothie game up a notch with this delicious Mango Pineapple Coconut Water Ninja Smoothie! Blended with sweet mangoes, juicy pineapple, and fresh coconut water, this is a refreshing treat is sure to please!
Serving: Serves 3-4
Preparation time: 5 minutes
Ready time: 5 minutes

Ingredients:
- 2 cups frozen mango
- 2 cups pineapple
- 2 cups coconut water
- 1 banana
- 2 tablespoons honey
- 1/2 teaspoon ground turmeric

Instructions:
1. Place frozen mango, pineapple, and coconut water in a blender and blend until smooth.
2. Add banana, honey, and turmeric and blend again.
3. Pour into glasses and enjoy!

Nutrition information: Calories: 170, Fat: 1.3 g, Cholesterol: 0 mg, Sodium: 17 mg, Carbohydrates: 41 g, Fiber: 3.7 g, Protein: 2.5 g

99. Raspberry Lime Basil Ninja Smoothie

This Raspberry Lime Basil Ninja Smoothie is the perfect way to start your day with a delicious kick of both sweet and savory flavor. It's easy to make and requires minimal Ingredients.
Serving: 1
Preparation Time: 5 minutes
Ready Time: 5 minutes

Ingredients:
- ½ cup raspberries
- ½ lime, peeled, with juice
- 5-7 large basil leaves
- ½ cup ice
- ¼ cup yogurt
- Honey, to taste (optional)

Instructions:
1. Place the raspberries, lime juice, basil leaves, ice, and yogurt into a blender and blend until smooth.
2. Adjust sweetness with honey, if desired, and blend again.
3. Run the smoothie through a strainer to remove any pulp.
4. Serve and enjoy.

Nutrition information:
Calories: 107 kcal, Carbohydrates: 21 g, Protein: 4 g, Fat: 1 g, Sodium: 18 mg, Potassium: 238 mg, Fiber: 3 g, Sugar: 11 g, Vitamin A: 98 IU, Vitamin C: 32 mg, Calcium: 86 mg, Iron: 1 mg

100. Matcha Banana Ninja Smoothie

Start your day with a delicious and nutritious Matcha Banana Ninja Smoothie! This smoothie features the energizing powers of matcha green tea and the sweet, creamy flavor of fresh banana. It's packed with omega-3s, fiber, and vitamins to keep you going.
Serving: 1
Preparation Time: 10 minutes
Ready Time: 10 minutes

Ingredients:

- 1 frozen banana
- ½ cup coconut milk
- 1 teaspoon matcha green tea powder
- 1 teaspoon honey or maple syrup
- 1 teaspoon chia seeds
- 5-6 ice cubes

Instructions:
1. Place all Ingredients in a blender and blend until smooth.
2. Pour into a glass and enjoy!

Nutrition information: Per serving: 175 calories, 8.1g fat, 22.2g carbohydrates, 2.2g fiber, 8mg sodium, 4.5g protein.

CONCLUSION

The Ninja Smoothie Revolution: 100 Recipes for Weight Loss and Increased Energy has demonstrated that smoothies are an effective and delicious way to lose weight and increase energy levels. From flavorful fruits and vegetables to energy-boosting nuts and seeds, the book has offered a collection of tasty and easy recipes that are great for busy lifestyles while taking into consideration dietary restrictions and preferences. The different recipes featuring superfoods such as chia seeds, kale, and acai have shown that there are endless possibilities for creating nutritious and delicious smoothies—making them perfect for anyone looking for some serious health benefits in their diet.

Overall, this cookbook is an excellent addition to anyone's kitchen, especially if you are looking to lose weight and increase energy levels. The recipes and techniques are simple and straightforward, allowing you to make your own smoothies in no time. With the right ingredients, you will be able to create a delicious and nutritious smoothie that can support your journey to a healthier and more energetic lifestyle.

What is more, the book is filled with useful tips, such as how to freeze smoothies for future use and how to store them properly. Furthermore, by using the different ninja recipes, you can even take the smoothies on the go. So why not start a healthy habit with smoothies today?

In summary, the Ninja Smoothie Revolution: 100 Recipes for Weight Loss and Increased Energy has presented a comprehensive collection of recipes and tips that are perfect for busy lifestyles. Whether it is for weight loss, increased energy levels, or just for general health benefits, this book will be able to help you enjoy the deliciousness and health benefits of smoothies all while not taking up too much of your time. So why wait? Try out some of these amazing smoothie recipes today!

Printed in Great Britain
by Amazon